Learn with Alex and Anna

Hello! We're, Alex and Anna. That's us with our dog Freddie and the rest of our family. Welcome to our series of books and stories.

We've been really busy doing lots of fun activities and we wanted to share some of our experiences with you, so Grandpa decided to write about them.

We have learnt lots of useful things from Grandpa, Grandma, Auntie Lucy, Mummy and Daddy, and Freddie has often been there to lend a helping paw too. Even though we've been learning new facts and information, we've been having so much fun, so none of it really felt like learning at all. We hope that through this book you will have just as much fun too.

You may need someone older to read this story to you to explain anything you might not understand. At the end of every story there are some questions for you to answer, so listen carefully. Some stories may have activities or experiments for you to carry out as well.

We want to thank you for getting this book and hope you enjoy reading it.

Have fun; we did.

Alex and Anna

Copyright © 2014 Peter Hayward
www.learnwithalexandanna.com
www.facebook.com/learnwithalexandanna

ISBN 13: 978-1505378191
ISBN 10: 1505378192

All rights reserved. No part of this publication may be reproduced, distributed, or transmitted in any form or by any means, including photocopying, recording, or other electronic or mechanical methods, without the prior written permission of the publisher or the author, except in the case of brief quotations embodied in critical reviews and certain other non-commercial uses permitted by copyright law.

Published by Alex and Anna Publishing
www.learnwithalexandanna.com

Quantity Sales: Special discounts are available on quantity purchases by corporations, associations, and others. For details contact Alex and Anna Publishing at the above website.

Acknowledgement

I'd like to say a very big thank you to Julie Day, my editor. Without her tremendous help I know that this book, and those that follow, would have fallen well short of the quality the children and parents reading them deserve.

I'd also like to thank Michael Barton, WordPlay and Wordplay Publishing Ltd, for his encouragement, advice and tireless assistance. Taking a vision and making it reality is a journey along a winding road. Michael helped straighten it.

This book is dedicated to my grandchildren, Ashley, Lilly and Emily. Life with them in it is truly inspiring.

One lazy Sunday morning everyone at Alex's house was relaxing, all except Alex. He was driving the whole family mad pedalling his car around the back garden as fast as he could. He drove over everything: clothes pegs, flowers, toys, Anna's dolls, and even Freddie's chew stick.

Anna was quietly sitting in the back garden puzzling over a puzzle when Alex suddenly headed straight for her. As soon as she realised what he was about to do, she let out a huge scream.

"Alex," Daddy sternly commanded from the kitchen doorway, "please don't drive into Anna. And, keep off the vegetable patch and the flowers too. They don't like getting run over by cars either."

"Okay, Daddy," Alex replied, as he swerved to avoid his sister just at the last second, grinning maniacally in the process.

Anna jumped out of the way in a huff.

Grandpa, who was enjoying a nice mug of coffee, decided to ease the situation. "Alex, do you want to come to the shops with me?" he asked.

"Yes, please," Alex answered excitedly, not realising that Grandpa had an ulterior motive. Nevertheless, going out with Grandpa on his own was fun because he always learnt something new. He quickly parked his car near the fence.

"I'll stay here now that I won't get run over," Anna sneered, sticking her tongue out at Alex.

Freddie the dog would have stuck his tongue out as well, but his mouth was full with his flattened chew stick.

Grandpa put his coat on and when they were both ready,

Alex and Grandpa strolled to the shops.

As they began their walk, Grandpa advised Alex that it wasn't nice to drive into Anna, or even over Freddie's chew stick. He then decided to educate Alex about road safety.

"Let's play a game where we learn things," Grandpa suggested.

"What game is that?" Alex asked. He liked Grandpa's games a lot because he always had fun playing them.

"It's the 'Let's keep safe on the footpath and the road' game," Grandpa replied, as they stepped onto the public path.

"How do you play that?" Alex asked, looking up at his grandpa quizzically; unsure what this game was.

"It's a game where we keep looking and listening for anything that comes along on the footpath or the road."

"Why would we do that?" Alex asked.

"I want you to be safe," Grandpa explained. "This footpath can be dangerous because it's used by both pedestrians and cyclists. Roads can also be dangerous if you don't know how to use them properly. And, back gardens can also be dangerous, especially if you drive into people."

Alex winced.

"So, we'll start with you walking on the inside of me," Grandpa continued. "Then there's less chance of you tripping into the road."

"Okay, Grandpa," Alex nodded in agreement.

Alex swapped sides with Grandpa so that Grandpa was nearest to the road.

"It also means holding my hand," added Grandpa, holding his hand out for Alex to take.

"Why?" Alex asked.

"Well, I might see something approaching that could be dangerous," Grandpa replied. "Then I can warn you."

"What things?" Alex asked.

"It could be anything," said Grandpa. "A car could suddenly appear from a driveway or a cycle being ridden too fast could suddenly run into you."

"I don't want to get run over," Alex replied.

"Nobody wants to get run over," Grandpa reminded Alex.

"Getting run over means you could get really hurt."

"I wouldn't want to run over anyone," Alex stated.

"Anna and her dolls don't like getting run over either," Grandpa remarked.

"Sorry," Alex replied, and he hung his head in shame.

"Perhaps when we get home, you can say sorry to Anna."

"I will," Alex replied.

Grandpa suddenly stopped and drew Alex closer to him. A cyclist riding on the footpath tore around the corner and nearly careered straight into them. It was lucky that Grandpa had spotted the cyclist as a high garden hedge had blocked Alex from sight. Even though the cyclist missed them, Alex jumped with fright, just like Anna had done earlier.

"Phew, that was close!" Alex exclaimed in relief.

"It was very close," Grandpa agreed. "I saw the cyclist coming. That's why we stopped."

"He could have run us over," Alex said.

"Yes, and we could have been hurt," Grandpa confirmed, "but luckily the cyclist saw us at the last moment. I'm sure he didn't intend to run over us, unlike when you were driving your car over Anna's dolls and Freddie's chew stick."

"Sorry," Alex repeated, bowing his head even lower this time.

"I'm glad you realise," Grandpa replied, looking at Alex out of the corner of his eye whilst trying to hide a small smile.

Continuing their walk Alex excitedly blurted out, "That's John's house." And he pointed to a house with a bike outside on the grass. "He's coming to see me after lunch."

"Cool," Grandpa replied. Grandpa like using cool words!

On their journey to the shops, they both stepped over cracks in the pavement to avoid falling into the centre of the earth. One time Grandpa caught the edge of one cracked path and was nearly dragged down, but Alex grabbed him and pulled him free.

They also jumped over drain covers just in case monsters grabbed their legs and pulled them into the bowels of the drainage system. Then they hopped onto a paving slab just to see if they could both fit. Alex also discovered that he sometimes got stuck to lampposts by a strange magnetic force which meant that Grandpa had to wrestle him free.

All the while, Grandpa pointed out places where accidents could happen, which included driveways to houses, especially those with high hedges or fences that blocked the view of passers-by. He taught Alex how to listen out for the noise from engines of vehicles, and how to spot reversing lights suddenly coming on. Grandpa also pointed out driver's blind spots as they passed cars, vans and trucks partially parked on the footpath. Blind spots are the areas that cannot be seen by the driver as they look forward or through either the rear-view or side mirrors.

Eventually they came to a point where they needed to cross the road, but there was no pedestrian crossing.

"Okay, Alex," Grandpa instructed, "let's stop a little way from the edge of the path before we cross."

"What for?" Alex asked, as they suddenly stopped.

"I'm going to teach you how to 'Stop, Look and Listen', before you cross the road," Grandpa explained.

"Is that a game?" puzzled Alex.

"No, it's not a game, Alex," Grandpa enforced. "This is serious now. We need to make sure the road is safe to cross. So, we must always stop, look and listen before we take our first step."

"My friends just run across the road," Alex pointed out.

"That could be dangerous because a passing driver might not have time to react and stop," Grandpa warned. "It is important to keep safe when crossing the road."

"But how do we do that?" Alex asked.

"First, we find a safe place to cross. A place where we can

see and be seen, and where there are no parked vehicles, trees or posts blocking us," Grandpa informed Alex. "Next, we stand away from the front edge of the path. Then, we take time to look around to check that the road is clear. Can you see anything?"

"Yes, I can see a car," Alex answered.

"Would it be safe to cross the road now?" Grandpa asked.

"No. That car would hit us." Alex replied.

"Well done," Grandpa praised Alex. "The car could hit us and we'd get hurt, so we let it pass."

"I don't want to get hurt," Alex stated.

"That's why before crossing a road we must choose a place which is safe and where people using the road can see us," Grandpa reinforced. "Then, we stop and stand away from the front edge of the path, just as we've done now. Next, we look around for traffic."

Another car whizzed by, its engine roaring.

"Is it safe to cross the road yet?" Grandpa asked again.

"No. I can see a bike coming this time."

"Well done," Grandpa credited him. "If we step out in front of a cyclist, we could still get knocked over or injured."

The cyclist passed and the road was clear.

"Now, we have to listen carefully," Grandpa instructed.

"Why?" Alex asked.

"To try to hear if there is anything coming that we can't see," Grandpa replied. "There may be a vehicle driving around the corner."

"Okay," Alex replied, he knew he was learning a lot today.

"So, we have stopped, we've looked, and now we're listening," Grandpa reminded Alex.

"Then, we can cross," Alex completed the sequence.

"Only when it's safe," Grandpa reinforced. "We can't see anything, but can you hear anything, Alex?"

"No," Alex replied.

"Okay, it's safe. Let's cross the road," Grandpa said. "But, we must keep looking and listening."

"Why?" Alex enquired.

"We must keep safe while we cross the road," Grandpa said. "We need to be alert all the time for anything that might appear unexpectedly. If it does, we can move forwards quicker or go back to the path we came from. But we must never run because we could trip over."

They both took a step into the road and briskly walked to the other side. All the while, they looked and listened for any approaching vehicles. Within seconds, they had safely crossed the road and were now standing on the opposite side.

"Well done, Alex," Grandpa congratulated his grandson.

All of a sudden, two children ran out from a nearby garden right in front of them. Without looking, the children ran straight into the road directly in front of a car travelling towards them. The car screeched to a halt, nearly hitting them. The two children just kept on running and disappeared into a garden opposite.

"They were really silly, Grandpa," Alex remarked. "They nearly got hit by that car."

"They were very lucky," Grandpa replied.

"They should have stopped and looked and listened," Alex stated.

"That's right," Grandpa agreed. "It's so simple and easy to be safe. All you need to do is 'Stop, Look and Listen' before you cross the road."

"You are so clever, Grandpa." Alex said.

"I'm just teaching you to be safe. You are my grandson and I care for you," Grandpa answered hugging Alex. "It's so simple and easy to learn and use 'Stop, Look and Listen'."

"Thank you, Grandpa," Alex beamed.

"Anna will also need to be taught how to cross the road safely," Grandpa suggested. "Perhaps you can teach her."

"I will," Alex smiled.

As they continued their journey towards the shopping centre Grandpa noticed that the roads were getting busier, so he gripped Alex's hand more firmly. Even so, they still managed to keep off the cracks in the pavement, just in case!

Through this part of their journey, they watched other pedestrians crossing the road, and with his new knowledge, Alex commented on those pedestrians who stopped, looked and listened, and those who didn't. Then crossing a few more roads themselves, Grandpa asked Alex to both show him and tell him what to do. Alex proudly instructed Grandpa to Stop, Look and Listen, before safely crossing the road.

Grandpa knew Alex was learning from this.

In due course, they came to a footpath where pedestrians and cyclists were separated. Keeping in the lane for pedestrians only, Alex and Grandpa eventually arrived at the shops.

After buying some delicious fresh cream cakes, Grandpa decided to take a different route home. This road was very busy with lots of traffic so Grandpa took extra care of his grandson.

They soon came to a crossing which was controlled by traffic lights: a pelican crossing. Alex immediately released his grip from Grandpa and started to run ahead.

"No, Alex," Grandpa commanded sternly. "Come back."

"But I want to push the button," Alex replied.

"I know you do," Grandpa replied less harshly, "but please stay beside me until you've learnt more about being safe."

Alex returned and took hold of Grandpa's hand again.

When they reached the crossing they stopped. Alex then pressed the button to operate the lights with extra force.

Next they stepped back away from the edge of the path and waited as lots of cars, buses, vans and trucks passed by in both directions. It would be very easy to fall under the wheels of a large truck if you were not being careful.

Soon the pelican lights facing the road changed to red for all vehicles to stop. Next, the 'green character' for pedestrians lit up, both on the sign on the opposite side of the road and on a sign next to the button Alex had pushed. A high-pitched beeping noise sounded too. This noise also notified pedestrians they could cross. Grandpa continued to hold Alex's hand as they briskly walked to the other side of the road.

"We must still look out for any vehicles," Grandpa reminded Alex.

"Why?" Alex, puzzled. "Everything's stopped."

"I know," said Grandpa, "but sometimes drivers miss the red lights and drive straight through them."

Having safely reached the other side of the road they headed for home. On their journey Alex saw other children his age walking with adults. One child dropped a ball and without looking, ran into the road to retrieve it. The adults with the child didn't seem to be concerned and didn't say anything.

"I'm glad you're my grandpa," Alex remarked, thinking about how much Grandpa had taught him today.

"I care for you and want to help you to learn to be safe," Grandpa said proudly.

Grandpa then noticed a young woman with earphones in her ears walking towards them along the footpath. A loud noise sounded from the earphones: music! The woman turned and suddenly stepped off the footpath straight into the road. Grandpa ordered Alex to stand still and not move. A millisecond later, he rushed towards the woman and pulled her back onto the footpath. At the same time, a lorry hurtled by, its horn blaring.

"You were nearly run over," Grandpa said to the youngster.

"Thank you," she said. "I'm sorry, I was listening to my music. I'm so grateful."

Grandpa returned to a smiling and proud Alex and they continued their walk home. Alex was even more alert now.

When they arrived home Daddy made them all a drink to go with the fresh cakes they were about to feast on.

As they all sat around the kitchen table Alex told everyone how he had learnt to 'Stop, Look and Listen'. He animatedly acted out how he had stopped, turned his head from side to side to demonstrate how he had looked, then put his hands to his ears to show how he had listened. When it was safe, he pretended to cross a road. All this whilst seated at the table.

Alex then apologised to Anna saying, "I'm sorry I nearly ran over you, Anna. When we next go out I'll teach you to cross the road safely."

"Thank you," Anna replied.

Daddy smiled and thanked Alex for offering to help his sister.

Later that afternoon, Alex's friend John and his mummy visited. Sitting in the back garden, Alex soon got bored with grown-ups' talk and went to the garden shed. Taking out his ride-on police car and tractor, Alex and John played in a world of their own.

Freddie was also bored and went for a walk. After a few circuits of the garden and finding no new smells, he saw food being brought out, so he trotted back to the adults. As he did so he wandered straight in front of Alex's police car.

"Whoa, Freddie," Alex shouted. "You didn't 'Stop, Look and Listen'."

"He didn't what?" asked a mystified John.

"Stop, Look and Listen," Alex repeated slowly. "Freddie just crossed in front of me."

"What's 'Stop, Look and Listen'?" John enquired.

"Before you cross the road, you have to stop, look and listen," Alex stated.

Grandpa heard Alex and said, "Alex, why don't you teach John and Anna how to cross the road safely?"

Daddy agreed and headed towards the garden shed.

He reappeared carrying some bamboo rods and wooden poles and laid them on the ground parallel to each other.

"We'll pretend that this is a road," Daddy instructed everyone, "and I'll pretend to be my work van. Alex you can teach Anna and John how to safely cross this pretend road."

Alex took hold of Anna's hand and stood on the pretend footpath, away from the pretend road, ready to cross. John stood beside them. Daddy positioned himself at the end of the poles and pretended to drive his work van along the pretend road. Grandpa then joined in, pretending he was a truck, while Mummy pretended to be a car and John's mummy pretended to be a bus. They all made different engine noises as they shuffled up and down the pretend road.

Alex then taught Anna and John how to 'Stop, Look, and Listen,' and to safely cross the pretend road. When they reached the opposite side, without harm, they turned around to cross back over again.

Freddie looked on wondering what on earth all these humans were doing. Grown-ups were waddling up and down between two sets of poles, making funny noises, while children kept stopping, looking and listening before moving forwards.

After a few more 'Stop, Look and Listens,' to make sure Anna and John had learnt how to safely cross a road, Daddy went into the kitchen to make them all a nice cup of tea. Everyone knew Daddy's tea was the best!

Alex and John returned to play in their own world whilst the parents sat and chatted, as they waited for their tea.

It was soon time for John and his mummy to leave. After saying their goodbyes, John and his mummy stepped onto the public footpath and came to a road which they had to cross.

"Mummy," John blurted out, "we need to 'Stop, Look and Listen' before we cross this road."

Having stopped, they looked in both directions. Next, they listened for any approaching vehicles. When the road was clear, they safely crossed, looking in both directions as they did so.

"Well done, John," Alex shouted. "You've learnt to stop look and listen."

"Thank you," John replied.

Grandpa smiled and said, "Alex teaches road safety."

Alex smiled proudly.

Learn with Alex and Anna

Hooray, you have just finished this story.

Let's see if you can answer these questions. Several of them require you to remember some of the important information and facts from the story.

1) What dangers should you look out for when you walk along a footpath?

2) Why should you walk on the pedestrian's side of a path shared with cyclists?

3) What are blind spots for drivers of vehicles?

4) Why should you stop, look and listen before you cross the road?

5) What dangers do you need to be aware of at a Pelican Crossing?

6) Who could get hurt if you cross a road in front of a vehicle?

An exercise for you.
Practice 'Stop, Look and Listen' every time you cross the road.

For more information on road safety contact your local council or visit
http://think.direct.gov.uk/education/early-years-and-primary

Thank you for reading our book and completing these questions.

We have other stories for you to read on different subjects.

Whatever you do, please try to be safe but have fun.

We did.

Don't forget, you can find out more at:

www.learnwithalexandanna.com
and
www.facebook.com/learnwithalexandanna

Alex and Anna

Other Books in the Series

(See website for publication details)

Alex and Anna's Acorn Helps the World

Alex the Firefighter Saves the Flowers

Grandpa's Train Journey

Seatbelt Safety

Chasing Shadows

Anna the Honeybee

BBQ Time

A Day at the Beach

Freddie the Wonder Dog

MY Mobile Phone

www.learnwithalexandanna.com

www.facebook.com/learnwithalexandanna

Learn with Alex and Anna

The remaining pages have intentionally been left blank for you to do some drawing and colouring or make notes.

Printed in Great Britain
by Amazon